Neighborhood Brands

Using the Internet and Social Media to Attract and Engage Local Customers

Jeff Farris & Dr. Alice Kendrick

BubbleLife Media
http://www.bubblelifemedia.com

Neighborhood Brands™

by Jeff Farris & Alice Kendrick

Printed in the United States of America

ISBN-10: 0615366317
ISBN-13: 978-0-615-36631-9

Published by:

BubbleLife Media LLC, 6805 Hillcrest Avenue, #208,
Dallas, TX 75205.

http://www.bubblelifemedia.com

Dedication

To Saffie Farris, the founder of
http://www.bubblelife.com.

Contents

Figures

Introduction

If you are reading this, you own or work for a neighborhood business. Chances are you are either using social media to connect with your customers, you're contemplating doing so, or it's on your to-do list along with a thousand other things competing for your attention. If you're already online, you may be worried about your rankings on Google and how to use Facebook or other social media to connect with your customers. This book is intended to de-mystify Internet tools, including social media, and to provide strategies and action plans that create, enhance or maximize your ability to attract and engage with local customers.

This book develops strategies based on the concept of a neighborhood brand. It helps you understand what a neighborhood brand is and why it is so important for your business. Social networking sites and Internet searches have changed the way customers begin their relationship with you. Customers are now more likely to find you through these activities than you are to find them through traditional advertising methods. A neighborhood brand is your way of ensuring that these changes benefit your business.

Before you say "I'm too busy" to get involved with new media, or to sharpen your current use of the Internet, consider that the practical guidelines proposed in this book will take you on average only 1-2 hours per week. And, most of the tools available to you are free.

Once you launch or refine your neighborhood branding efforts for communicating with your customers and prospects, maintaining those efforts is something that won't bankrupt your schedule or your pocketbook. In fact, many business owners tell us that they actually enjoy and look forward to their new way of communicating with customers. Not only does it feel right, but it also allows them to achieve marketing goals without resorting to expensive and often ineffective advertising tactics they've employed in the past.

Strategy Before Implementation

Too many times websites and social media solutions are implemented without any strategy behind them. Using Facebook or Twitter by themselves will not transform your business, but the use of web tools with a solid neighborhood branding strategy can put you in a "space" with customers that traditional media such as newspapers and radio never could.

This guide is written for a neighborhood business whose market is determined by the location of its front door. It helps define a strategy based around:

1. Using web content targeted at search engines and local customers to build a neighborhood brand.
2. Leveraging social networks and neighborhood communities to accelerate that brand.

This guide explains the issues so a business can move forward with implementation. It does this by answering these questions:

1. What is a neighborhood brand?
2. Who are my Internet-enabled customers?
3. What is content and how do you get it in front of readers?
4. How can the Internet help build a neighborhood brand?
5. How you can integrate Internet and offline efforts?

The last chapter of this book ties everything together and provides an implementation checklist. Most of the steps are either free or less expensive than what most businesses are doing now. By reading this book, you will learn that building a neighborhood brand is about where you spend your time and how you engage with customers.

Additional Resources

As you go through this book, remember to visit the book's companion website http://www.neighborhoodmarketing101.com for more information. There you will find downloadable copies of worksheets, links to web resources, additional articles, suggested readings and other materials that assist you in applying the lessons from this book.

What is a Neighborhood Brand?

When I first moved to my neighborhood 20 years ago everyone knew that Kuby's was where you bought your meat, Weir's was where you bought furniture and Culwell's sold the nicest clothes. I'm not sure any of this was from advertising; it was just common neighborhood knowledge.

In traditional marketing terms this is known as word of mouth. In "modern" terms it might be called viral marketing, network effect or buzz marketing. But, whatever you call it, it works. Local companies acquired their brand through longevity. I'm not sure if Kuby's, Weir's or Culwell's were known more than 10 miles from their front door and I'm not sure they cared. Their market was primarily five miles from their front door, so anything extra was nice but not essential.

Note: Time helps. Kuby's is the baby of the bunch launching in 1961. Weir's started in 1948 and Culwell's opened its doors in 1920.

In the age of the Internet, neighborhood brands have become the only way a local business can compete against larger chains and online retailers. Fortunately the Internet not only enables local businesses to develop a neighborhood brand but also gives them the tools to build their brand much faster than the multi-generational neighborhood brands mentioned above.

Before getting into how to build a neighborhood brand, let's spend a little time getting to understand what a neighborhood brand is.

Neighborhood Brands are Stories

A neighborhood brand is recognition among residents that a particular business excels at delivering a product, selection, service or experience. In other words a neighborhood brand means that:

> **When locals think of _____ they immediately think of _____ (fill in the blanks with your particulars).**

More importantly, a neighborhood brand means that:

> **When friends ask about _____, people immediately mention _____ (again fill in the blanks with your particulars).**

Okay, the last paragraph may be a little simplistic, but the key point is that a neighborhood brand is defined by your customer, not by you. It is the direct result of bundles of experiences with your brand, whether direct or indirect. And while you may shape your brand, your customer defines it. Some of the elements that you control that influence your brand include:

- Information you provide
- Your company's staff
- How customers are greeted
- How often you communicate with customers
- How you communicate with customers
- Customer service
- Products and services
- Location
- Store policies, hours, guarantees
- Store or office appearance
- The look and feel of your business or product
- The smell and sound of your business
- Community involvement
- Niche
- Advertising and promotion

These elements translate into stories that a person can use to explain your brand to someone else. For example, "I was rushed to put together a special dinner and the nice people down the street at Kuby's helped me pick out four of the best steaks I've ever tasted." Brands with great stories have an easier time catching on or gaining traction.

Neighborhood Brands Are Top of Mind/Tip of Tongue

When someone asks "where's the best place to get ice cream?" or "do you know any good plumbers?," the mental list that pops into the respondent's head is called an evoked set. Some of the most telling evidence about whether a brand has traction among its target audience is to examine the content of these consumer responses. Not only do customers recall a handful of brands, but they rank them, whether or not they have ever said that ranking out loud.

Where's a good place for a hamburger?

1. Burger House
2. Jimmie's Burgers
3. Fuddruckers
4. McDonald's

Figure 1 – Evoked Set of Responses

Occupying space on these mental ladders that consumers carry around in their heads is the result of either personal experience, word of mouth, news stories or brand promotion. Nothing can trump personal experience with a brand in terms of customer attitudes, but not everyone has experienced your product. It is likely that many potential customers formulate impressions of your brand based solely on what they hear, read or see about you. Therefore, effective articles, messaging and stories in places where customers will see and read them is essential to your neighborhood brand's success.

Neighborhood Brands are Niches

An important element of neighborhood branding is niche. A neighborhood niche is the product or service you offer, seen through neighborhood eyes. The smaller the niche, the better the brand and the easier it is for the neighborhood to remember your stories.

For example, the following categories suggest a greater level of niche or focus as you proceed from a general concept to a more tightly refined one:

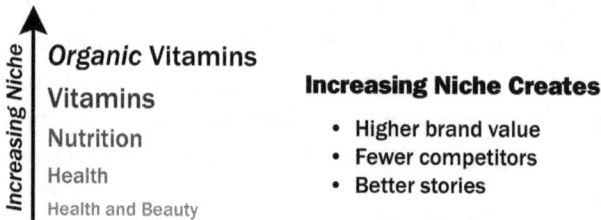

Organic **Vitamins**

Vitamins

Nutrition

Health

Health and Beauty

Increasing Niche ↑

Increasing Niche Creates

- **Higher brand value**
- **Fewer competitors**
- **Better stories**

Figure 2 – Increasing Niche

As focus increases, a brand becomes stronger and the number of businesses or competitors at each level decreases in both the neighborhood and in the online world. This is an important point. At the health and beauty level, chains like Walgreen's and CVS fit as do online merchants such as drugstore.com. By the time you move to a higher level of focus you are now starting to think more about companies such as the local GNC or health food store.

The key here is that if you are trying to create a neighborhood brand by competing in a broader category, it will be more difficult. You'll be a small player with a small neighborhood market share. But as you begin to create a niche for your business, you become a bigger player with a bigger market share and that's easier for your customers to respect and remember.

Most large categories are already taken by one, or a small handful of big business names.

- Best general bookstore
- Best place to buy Apple computers
- Best general drug store

However for every large or general category that is unavailable to the local business, there are many more category specialties that are easy to promote in a neighborhood such as:

- Best Southwest style Mexican food
- Best live jazz
- Best place to have a beer with friends
- Best place to go with a broken computer
- Best realtor for selling a contemporary house
- Best coffee house for meetings
- Best bookstore for small kids
- Best place to buy used Apple computers
- Best drugstore for seniors

A neighborhood brand is about stories, and niches make it easier for people to remember and repeat the stories that ultimately enhance your reputation and your sales. For example, when was the last time you were asked "Where should I go for food?" versus "Where should I go for good Chinese food?" People think and speak about shopping, dining and services in terms of niches.

Refining your Neighborhood Niche

It seems safer to be all things to all people so that you don't miss out on any sale. But when you try being all things you compete with more and larger companies for mindshare with customers. When you "niche down" your number of direct competitors decreases and it is much easier to create mindshare.

If you haven't recently, you may want to consider what your ideal niche might be. You should determine whether your concept of your current niche is in sync with what your customers or prospects think. Then, you need to contrast your niche with that of your competitors using a table similar to the example shown on the next page.

	Does Well	Does Different
Me	• Taste & Freshness	• Family Owned • Multi-generation • Seasoned fries
Competitor 1	• Clean • Consistent	• Drive Through • Playground
Competitor 2	• Broad Menu	• Beer and Wine • Sports TV

Figure 3 – Competitive Niche Analysis

Use your own version of the comparison to refine your niche. The more you can differentiate yourself from larger and smaller competitors, both online and down the street, the more your customers can create stories that drive your brand.

Neighborhood Brands Dominate Share of Voice

Share of voice (SOV) is an important consideration for any brand. It basically means how visible or audible your business is in the marketplace. Are you being heard "out there?" Are you being seen and heard as much as your competitors? The assumption is that the more you communicate your business message, the more people will see it. The typical thinking is that the more you spend, the more times your message gets said and the more people will listen. It's important to consider your surroundings when determining an appropriate 'volume' of marketing communications for a neighborhood brand. You don't want your brand to be an annoying neighbor, but you do want to be seen and heard.

SOV used to be defined by the amount of dollars spent in places like newspaper, radio, television and magazines. You have experienced valiant attempts at increasing SOV when you see the same television commercial multiple times in a single night's viewing. If you're like most people, unless the message is extraordinarily entertaining, you start to tune it out after you've heard it a few times. Sometimes you wish you could say "shut up already!" But you can't. Again, you don't want your brand messaging to be like that, and it doesn't have to.

As a small business, you have many more options for increasing share of voice in a way that doesn't resemble a shouting match. The good news about neighborhood brands is that they don't have to communicate all the way across a metropolitan area, state or country. The most important talking — and listening — you can do is within close range of your place of business — to your neighbors. And unlike traditional SOV that was amassed via enormous amounts of ad purchases for one-way communication, neighborhood brands don't have to lay out vast amounts of money to communicate effectively with customers. When you do communicate, much of it is a dialogue rather than a monologue, thanks to social media.

Old Method for Share of Voice ($$$$)   **New Method** ($-Free)

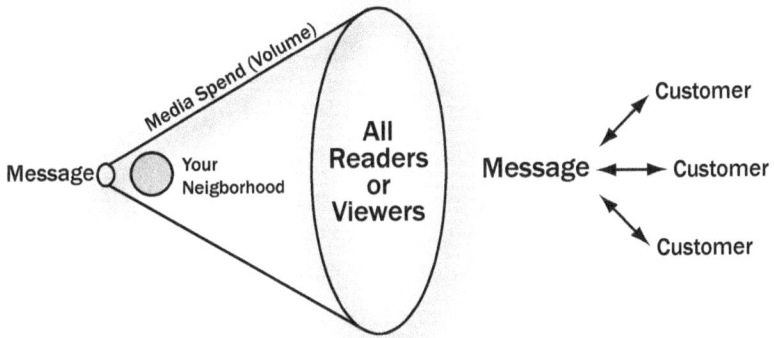

Figure 4 – Share of Voice

A good example of marketing share of voice occurs every time we attend a sporting event. The announcer "shouts" at us through the sound system so maybe we'll be able to hear above the noise. But, we don't need a sound system to talk to our friend sitting next to us. If share of voice is measured by comparison based on big media megaphones such as newspapers or television, we have to shout to be heard and we reach a lot of people we probably don't even want to reach. When talking to those closest to us, those in the neighborhood, a conversational voice is actually much better.

What Happens When You Stop

Anyone who has ever watched children knows that you often worry more when things get quiet than when things are noisy. Noise means activity. Happy noise means happy activity. No noise means we don't know what's going on. It's an unknown. Business SOV is the same way. Good noise means good things. Quiet means an unknown. When businesses are "noisy" and then go quiet, customers are left wondering what's happening. A consistent effort in a reasonable voice helps customers know you are still around and "happy".

Neighborhood Brand: The Formulas

You can understand neighborhood branding with two basic formulas:

1. **Neighborhood Brand = Name + Niche + Consistency + Engagement**

2. **Neighborhood Brand = Stories**

For the mathematically oriented, you can also express this as:

Stories = Name + Niche + Consistency + Engagement

Combining your name, niche and consistency (or quality) of product or service gives customers fodder for the stories they need to explain your brand to their friends. The Internet and social media give you opportunities to connect with your customers, which further connect them to your brand and facilitate their communication to others about your brand or in the presence of your brand message. Those connections and the increased involvement of your customers constitute engagement. When your customers pass along your stories to their neighborhood friends then you hold the distinction of a successful neighborhood brand.

It is estimated that the product or service you offer accounts for a mere 20% of what your brand is worth. Many aspects of products and services on the market are easily duplicated. The 80% of your brand equity that is in addition to and enhances a product or service in the eyes of your customers and potential customers is what we'll focus on next. Now that you better understand what a neighborhood brand is, let's explore how you can build or enhance your brand in months rather than over generations, using the Internet. We'll start by understanding the Internet-enabled customer.

Who are My Internet-Enabled Customers?

Even if your business doesn't have a website, you are still dealing with Internet-enabled customers. These are customers who, rather than turn to the yellow pages or local newspaper, now turn to the web or to their online network of friends for help finding the businesses they deal with. Then, they use the web to learn more about that business before calling or visiting and may even use the web to research competitors or alternatives. The Internet-enabled customer is a fact even if you sell haircuts, art classes, automotive repairs or other goods or services that are not considered Internet related.

Because of services like Google and devices like iPhones, Internet-enabled customers do not have to invest a great deal of time to become smarter consumers. Useful information is just a few clicks or seconds away.

The Internet-enabled consumer is transforming the way businesses reach customers. Methods such as direct mail, newspaper advertising and sales calls are less effective because customers now would rather find information on their own or from friends than have a "stranger" influence their choices. Then, even if they would be receptive to traditional marketing, the Internet-enabled customer is more likely spending their reading time online.

In order to better engage with the Internet-enabled customers, you must have a clear picture of:

1. Who is a customer?
2. What customers do you want?
3. How those customers engage with you online?

Using this information, it becomes much simpler to develop the right tactics for implementing Internet tools and social media.

First, Who is a Customer?

In order to understand the Internet customer, you first start with a good understanding of who your customers are. In general, customers are identified by four different types of characteristics that can be broken down by:

- Location
- Attributes
- Needs
- Behaviors

As you come to define these characteristics of your customer, you can better direct your Internet tactics. The best way to build your customer profile is by asking. Don't be afraid to engage with a customer in a more meaningful dialogue. While it may not be polite to ask their income, it is always fair to ask questions such as:

- Where did you hear of us?
- Did you visit our website before coming?
- Do you have children in school?
- Where do you spend your volunteer time?
- Do you use Facebook?
- Where do you get your local news?
- Do you think your friends might be interested?

Again, the more you know about your customer, the more likely you'll not only get them back but also more customers just like them. If you have difficulty getting information from customers, consider offering them something of value for the information such as an immediate discount or free accessory. Depending on your business, a weekly or monthly raffle is a great way to get business cards or survey information.

If needed, you can structure your information collection through the use of printed questionnaires. Be sure to ask only for the information that would be helpful to your business and don't ask for any information on a printed form that you wouldn't ask for face-to-face.

Location

For a neighborhood business, location is driven by where your front door is situated. Obviously there are hundreds of millions of Internet users, but for your neighborhood business all that really matters are those who live or work nearby. Sometimes this is referred to as your "five mile world".

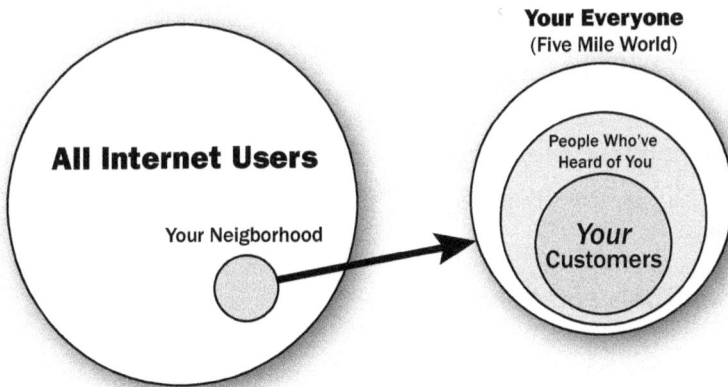

Figure 5 – Five Mile World

There are many advantages to having customers just a few miles from your front door including:

- Formation of relationships
- Face-to-face discussions and feedback
- Capability to provide immediate gratification
- Ability to demonstrate and showcase products
- Easier to cross-sell other items
- Familiar faces

Online, you'll want to focus your efforts to maximize these advantages while also targeting your efforts as precisely as possible to those within your five mile world.

Attributes

Even within your five mile world, there is a mix of people not all of whom are a good fit for your business. For example, a landscaper may not find many prospects among college kids. Defining more attributes about a typical customer helps you target your efforts to the most likely audience. Attributes you should know about your customer include:

- Age
- Gender
- Housing status (buy, rent)
- Family makeup (young kids, older kids, no kids)
- Type of employment

These attributes can be used to tailor your messaging, graphical design and placement of online efforts. For example, if you are targeting families with young children, content designed to appeal to mothers may be the most appropriate.

Customer Goals and Needs

Customers have many goals based on their perceived needs. Once you understand the location and background of your customers, then you can start to identify these needs such as:

- Educational activities for children
- Clothing requirements for work
- Time available for dining

Needs should match with your product or service and help you create new products or services or tailor existing ones. On the Internet, needs help you drive promotions and calls to action.

Customer Behaviors

Lastly, you'll need to understand more about what your customers do with their time and where they get and share information. You need to understand things such as:

- How far do they commute to work?
- Where to they spend their volunteer time?
- How often do they schedule activities?
- Which media do they use?
- What do they use media for, such as entertainment, news, etc.?
- Which media do they use to search for information about businesses, products and services?
- What online sites do they visit?
- How often do they participate on Facebook?
- Do they use iPhones or other email capable smartphones?

Behaviors help you understand how you can tap into customers' daily lives to reach them with your information. There are many places you can put your ads and other content. The best places fit well into existing customer behaviors.

What Customers Do You Want?

In most cases the type of customer you had yesterday is the type of customer you want tomorrow. But sometimes as businesses are adapting to changing markets or competition, it is helpful also to ask "What customers would I like to have tomorrow?" If the answer is different than the type you have today, you will need to rework the answers from above into the persona of the customer you want and act accordingly.

How Do Customers Engage Online?

On the Internet, customers are classified based on their engagement with your business. At each stage of engagement, customers have different needs that must be met for them to engage further. These stages and needs are shown in the following figure.

Engagement Level	Method of Engagement	Test
Seeker – Has a need or curiosity and is researching solutions and alternatives.	Search engine, Ad (banner ad, content)	Must be findable
Gatherer – Has identified your business as a possible solution to a perceived need.	Information and content (blog, success stories, white papers)	Must build trust
Lead – Identifies himself or herself to your business as a potential customer.	Call to action (invitation, event, promotion)	Must be able to deliver
Customer – A repeat customer if satisfied and engaged.	Follow-up, Mind share (email, phone call)	Must be a consistent presence
Loyal Customer – A regular customer who spends a majority of his or her "category dollars" with you. Loyal customers may not tell everyone about you, but they keep coming back.	Experience and validation	Consistency
Maven – A person who routinely tells others about your exceptional product or service.	Stories	Very positive Experiences

Figure 6 – Levels of Engagement

Customers move to higher levels when they acquire more information and higher confidence in your business. More importantly, customers become more valuable. At the maven level they represent an unpaid and highly trusted informal sales force for your prospects.

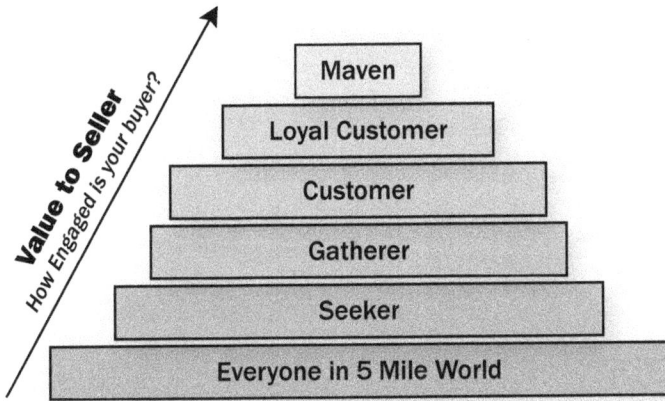

Figure 7 – Increasing Value of Engagement

Neighborhood businesses should have a plan that facilitates and encourages customers to move from the seeker level to the maven level. If you start engaging but fail to keep up your efforts, customers fall to the bottom in terms of value.

It takes money to reach and find those potential customers who have never heard of you. But once you've found them, it pays to engage directly. The cost to call, mail or email is considerably less. Tools such as email can make it almost free to reach your most valuable customers and mavens.

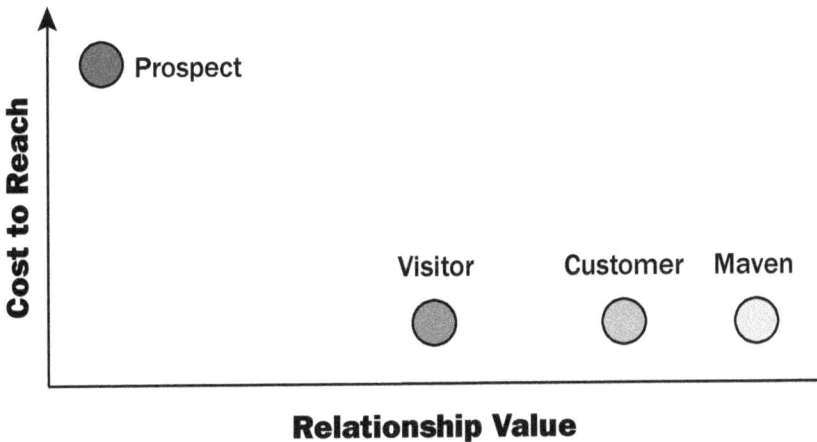

Figure 8 – Cost to Reach vs. Value

Increasing customer levels of engagement is good for growing revenues and reducing expenses. Almost all high-end or high-ticket businesses have used customer engagement even before the Internet. Now, the Internet makes these proven techniques work for any size business no matter what the average transaction amount. The next two chapters lay out the details.

What is Web Content?

Before going into the detail of what Internet tools you should use for building your neighborhood brand, we first need to explain the basic building block of the web – content. From a business perspective, content is a broad category that includes any information on the web about your business. When a business launches a website, contributes to a blog or otherwise provides information online it basically becomes a publisher of content. Your customers also create content about your business any time they post a review or discuss your business online with their friends.

Content can be text or it can be photos, videos or audio files. The structure and design in which the information is presented are also considered content. The expression "content is king" refers to the fact that without this original material to attract people to the web, there would be nothing but advertising.

For businesses trying to attract and engage customers, not all content is considered equal. Content that is relevant to the type of customers you want is much more valuable than that which is less relevant. Of this content, text content is the fastest to create, the easiest to produce and the simplest to publish. And, as we will discuss next, it is also the easiest for search engines to work with. Text content can also be reused in other ways. For example, a blog post could become the basis for any number of other efforts.

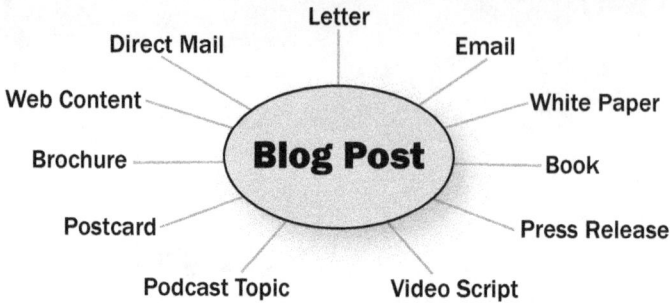

Figure 9 – Blog Post Uses

Web content is the primary way a prospect comes to know a business and it is the primary way a business can build trust with the prospect. It is also a great starting point for any other type of marketing activity. However, just placing content online doesn't mean that search engines will find it or customers will read it. To make this clearer, it helps to understand the basics of how Internet search engines work.

How Do Search Engines Work?

Search engines, like Google, work on the concepts of content and authority. For search engines, content is the words that appear on a web page or in the files stored on your website. Authority is the number of other websites that reference your web page or content. The links from other websites also have their own authoritative scores which are also reflected in the search results. For example, a link from the New York Times or Wall Street Journal has more authority than a link from a local website. Search engines are constantly reading web pages and building indexes of content weighted by their authority. In short:

Content (think words) + Authority (think links from other websites) = Ranking

Of course, there are some complications. Searches based on words or phrases that frequently occur and in numerous places, such as "insurance", are harder for search engines to get right than searches based on words that seldom occur, such as "bubblelife".

An important point to remember in creating content is that content needs to feature words people use as search terms. For example, you might refer to your business as a "technology troubleshooting" company. However, most people search for "computer repair". If your content uses your phrase rather than the more typical search phrase, your content will seldom, if ever, appear in any search results.

There are numerous criteria that search engines use to try to get the right results. With the exception of one, almost all work against a local business. That exception is location.

Location, Location, Location

Every time you make a connection to the Internet, whether from your computer or phone, your computer is assigned a unique "address", also called an IP address, so that other computers can talk to your computer. These addresses are not random, but are assigned based on who is providing the service. Since these addresses have providers and these providers have physical addresses, it is possible for search engines to know your approximate location and tailor their results accordingly. Even basic searches are starting to reflect this.

Google has the ability to refine searches with the "Nearby" tool in the Search Options panel. One of the really helpful things about this tool is that it works geographically — not just with keywords — so users don't have to worry about adding "Dallas" to a query and missing web pages that only say "Plano" or "DFW."

For neighborhood businesses, the "Nearby" search option starts to tilt the advantage back to local businesses as opposed to the national online businesses typically favored in past Google searches. For local businesses, these localized results give them an ability to rank in search engines better than larger companies using high-priced search engine specialists.

Location is becoming an increasingly important part of the way Google searches. For anyone looking for a restaurant, automotive service, dry cleaning, dentistry or any other product or service delivered in the neighborhood, location is vital to finding the right information.

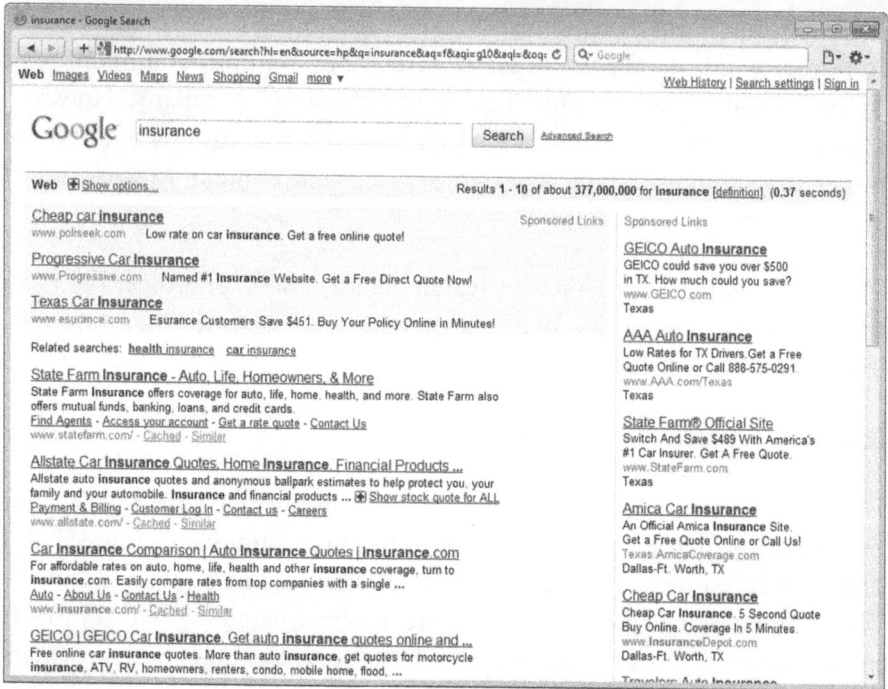

Figure 10 – Google Search for Insurance

The figure above shows a typical search for "insurance" which returns a list of national insurance companies with no local context including:

- State Farm
- Allstate
- Geico
- Farmers

Many users, frustrated with national search results for a local need, are increasingly using the search term "near" in their search which tells the search engine to tailor its result to a specific location. Searches for "insurance" and "insurance near 75205" return very different results as the figure on the next page shows.

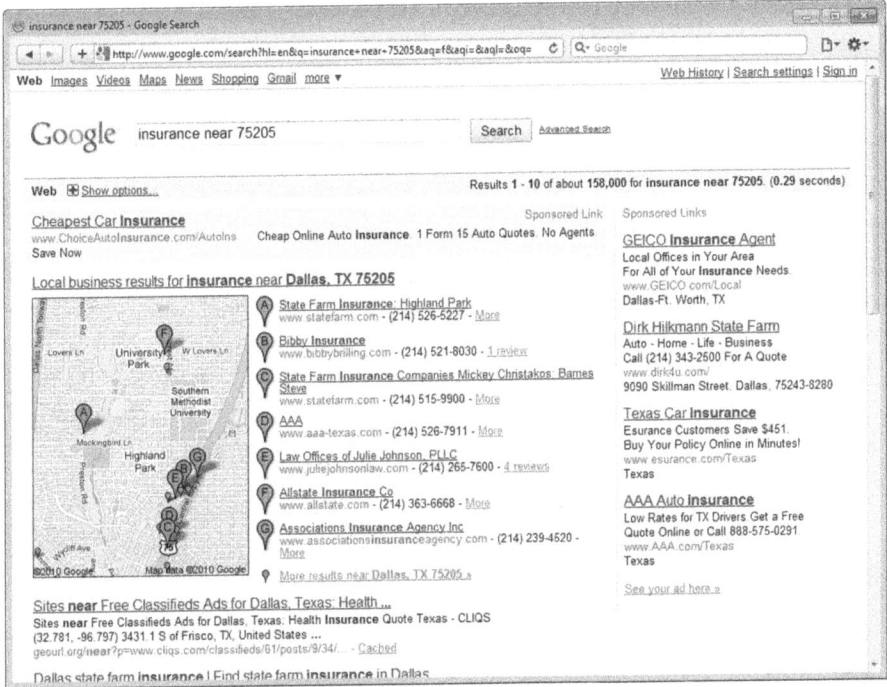

Figure 11 – Google Search for Insurance Near 75205

With the near option, the search results show the national company names but also provide a map showing the address of local agents.

Search Types

Searching is a broad concept. People search for different types of content based on their knowledge and familiarity with their topic. Searches can include:

- Category searches – shoes, jeans, insurance
- Parent brand searches – Nike, Levis, State Farm
- Branded product searches – Nike Air, Levi's 501, State Farm auto insurance
- Branded services searches – Southwest Airlines, Great Clips, Cowboy Cab
- Competitor searches – Lane's Shoes, Nordstrom, Just for Feet

- Geographic searches – shoes near University Park, shoes near 75205
- Business searches – Computer Corner, Apple Store, Best Buy

Online, these searches can be done using search engines search as Google or through friends using questions on websites such as "Where's a good place to get running shoes?"

Learn From the Search Long Tail

Usually, when people search on the web for information, they start with a general search and then keep adding words until they get a list of results they want. For example, a successive list of searches might be:

1. Insurance
2. Home insurance
3. Condo insurance
4. Condo insurance near Dallas

Not surprisingly, the word "insurance" gets searched for a lot more times on Google each day than the phrase "Condo insurance near Dallas". In fact it's a lot more times – by a factor of 100,000 or more. What is surprising is that each day, more than half of the searches on Google are unique for that day. That means when you search for "red shoes for Halloween costume near Dallas", that out of millions of search queries submitted that day, yours was unique.

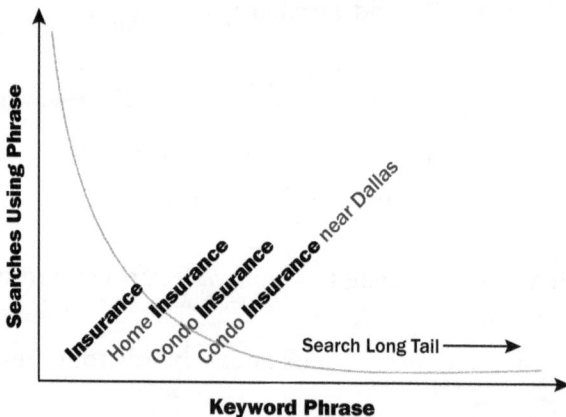

Figure 12 – Search Long Tail

The phrase "long tail" describes the phenomenon that there are a lot of unique searches for every popular search. Depicted in graph form, it looks like a long tail.

To maximize searchability, content needs to work toward both the larger search terms but also address the narrower terms as well. In other words, content about a very specific topic has a good chance of being searched for and listed in the search results.

Google provides a great free tool to help you visualize the number of searches based on keywords and related keyword matches. See the Resources section on the website http://www.neighborhoodbrands.com for a link to this tool and others.

Search Engine Optimization – Simpler than it Sounds

The term "search engine optimization" or SEO is an industry term that translates into making your content easily findable through searches. Getting the best search results for a small business does not have to be difficult and does not require great expense. To get good search results, businesses should:

- Have a dedicated website or some place that aggregates their information
- Produce lots of good content mentioning words that users would use to search
- Ensure that each page has a good title and use the page meta tags (in the page's HTML) to properly describe the content and add a few more terms for the search engines to read
- Include the business address including city, state and zip code on every page
- Err on the side of text. Search engines don't really care how your website or content looks. They work on words, not style.
- Most importantly, get the site URL or business name mentioned on other websites through reviews, public relations, customer feedback, comments on other blogs and any other effort you have time for.

Unfortunately, it's difficult to accomplish great results with a single web page. To make these points more clear, we'll focus in on content and its placement.

Content: For People and Search Engines

You can think of content in two forms — user friendly content and search engine friendly content. User friendly content is written with brevity and clarity and sometimes implied context. This is the opposite of what search engines like. Search engines like text and lots of it. There are two ways to approach this problem: write search engine friendly articles that users won't read, or write lots of user friendly content that, in total, addresses the needs of the search engines. Obviously, the latter is the only compromise that works. The good news is that content isn't just a long article. Content includes:

- Educational stories
- Success stories
- Information and pictures of your products
- Pictures and names of your staff
- Product tips
- Product guides
- Pictures of your store interior or exterior
- List of upcoming events
- Interviews with customers
- Sales coupons or other promotions
- Upcoming events
- Links to other web sites
- Files containing forms or product manuals
- Advertisements
- Directory entries
- Twitter posts
- Facebook posts
- LinkedIn status updates
- Plus a lot more…

This content includes item titles, subtitles and side text. Every piece of text helps with search engines. The more content you create, the more content search engines have to index and rank.

Where Do I Put This Content?

Once you have content, the next step is to put it where it gets the most results. You have a number of options, and content can be placed in more than one of them. The more common choices include:

- Your website
- Your business blog
- Comments to others' blogs and discussions
- Neighborhood websites
- Email
- Social Media like Twitter and Facebook
- Press releases

In the next section of this book, we will explain in more detail what these different online tools are and how best to use them.

It's important to remember that not all of the places listed above have to be on your website. In fact, it is often better that they reside at different places to increase a search engine's perception of authority. But remember that not all of these choices generate the same results. Google keeps track of more than one trillion unique URLs and for success you need your prospects and customers to visit yours. When getting started the best rule is to place your content and references to your content where your prospects and customers already are:

1. Advertise your website or blog in your store or reception area
2. Place your content where your prospects and customers are going already
3. Place your content where you can stand out among other businesses already there
4. Check out neighborhood websites that already reach your targeted customers

Generating content and placing it in multiple places following the rules above generates the best results. The following table summarizes some of your choices.

Website

Pros

- Complete ownership of look and content
- Cumulative effect of content increases branding
- Provides home for online presence
- Improves search results

Cons

- May not have many visitors
- May contain stale content
- Expensive startup

Business Blog

Pros

- Inexpensive
- Provides content that is continually updated (dynamic)
- Enhances expertise
- Builds brand
- Improves search results

Cons

- Takes time to create content

Neighborhood Website

Pros

- Already generates traffic
- Focused audience
- Easier to stand out
- May provide other tools for customer engagement

Email

Pros

- Inexpensive
- Good for specials and promotions
- Great for direct contact

Cons

- Competes with SPAM in the inbox
- Requires advance permission
- Associated with hard sell
- Low response rates to bulk emails

Social Media

Pros

- Inexpensive
- Easy to use

Cons

- May not be relevant
- Need to build base of fans or followers
- Easy to overuse

Internet Advertising

Pros

- Creates awareness
- Generates traffic to website or landing page

Cons

- Moderate price
- Requires graphics
- Requires good call to action
- Wasted viewership if outside your targeted area
- Requires landing page or website

Press Release

Pros

- Gives credibility when reprinted
- Adds to web content

Cons

- No audience targeting
- Expensive
- Takes time
- Lack of editorial control

Persistent and Disposable Content

Content can be thought of as either persistent or disposable. Persistent content maintains its value to readers over time. Disposable content has a limited time value. For example, content that talks about how to get wine stains out of shirts would be considered persistent. Content that provides a coupon for 20% off of dry cleaning through Saturday would be considered disposable. Disposable content is good at motivating actions but is not good at building trust. Persistent content is good at building trust but may not be good at generating immediate actions. To be effective, a business's content should be a mix of both. Some examples are shown on the next page.

Disposable Content

- 50% Off This Weekend Only
- Buy 1 Get 1 Free
- President's Sale Promotion

Persistent Content

- How to Choose the Right Skis
- Changing Fashions on the Slope
- Choosing the Right Ski Destinations for Families

Once you separate your content into disposable or persistent, you should then review where each should go and where it maximizes customer trust and activity. The following table outlines an approximate breakdown of how much content should be of one type or the other for each web placement.

Web Content Placement	Persistent and Disposable Mix
Website	90% persistent, 10% disposable (special offers on home page)
Business Blog	100% persistent
Neighborhood Website	Any mix but disposable content should not dominate frequency
Email	Any mix but persistent emails should look considerably different from disposable emails
Social Media	90% persistent for getting forwards among social network, 10% disposable for exceptionally compelling calls to action
Internet Advertising	50% persistent for branding awareness, 50% disposable for calls to action
Press Releases	100% disposable (see note below)

Figure 13 – Persistent and Disposable Content Mix

Note: Press releases are shown as disposable and this is true when considering the timeframe of the press release. However, for web purposes, press releases should be considered more like blog posts that present a history of the business and its accomplishments. Press releases typically play an important role in building a business' searchable web content because they mention specific people, customers, products, features and services that may themselves be the subject of a web search.

How Can the Internet Help Build a Neighborhood Brand?

It's taken a few pages to get here, but now it's time to start applying what we've talked about in the book. People ultimately define your brand, but you can use the Internet to help them define it in a way that is the closest to what you want. Using Internet tools and techniques you can both create your brand for customers and encourage customers to spread (or accelerate) your brand.

Create

- Awareness – Use advertising, content, public relations and search engines to make people aware of your brand
- Identity – Use websites and blogs to help define who you are and what you do best
- Confidence – Use quality educational content to enhance your reputation and trust

Accelerate

- Push – Use email and social networks to 'get the word out' with announcements or to let people know about new content

- Engagement – Use email, blog comments and other two-way methods of communication to engage customers in conversations
- Amplification – Make it easy for users to share your stories with their neighborhood

There are Internet tools that you develop and have greater control of and there are those that are used by your customers that you have much less control over. The first group we'll label content tools because they are driven by the content you create. The second group we'll label social networking tools because they are more driven by the way that people use them rather than by what you write. These are the tools that can accelerate your brand. Through this continual process of creation and amplification, you can encourage people toward your neighborhood brand goal so that when locals think of _____, they think of your business.

Content Tools

There are many places to put your content on the Internet and it's easy to get distracted with the latest fad. However, there are some basics that customers and search engines expect. These include:

- Your website
- Your business blog
- Web advertising
- Web public relations
- Social networking

Each plays an important role in engaging your customers. Although time usually prohibits addressing all simultaneously, it is most beneficial when a business can employ each type to engage customers.

Your Website

Your website is viewed by your customers as your storefront on the Internet. And, just like a storefront, a website communicates the personality and characteristics of your business even before customers walk in the front door. Your website should:

- Clearly communicate what you do

- Help stress your key branding messages
- Stress your ties to the neighborhood
- Create trust
- Add to your reputation
- Provide stories for people to communicate to one another
- Be helpful
- Help you to be found in search engines

It should feature:

- Basic information about your business
- Dynamic content such as a list of recent blog posts, news items or upcoming events
- Links to your other web locations such as your blog, Facebook fan page or Twitter updates
- Calls to action for joining email list, blog, fan page or Twitter following
- Information that helps customers

A checklist is provided in Appendix A that can help make sure your website has the content your customers expect.

Business Blog

One of the general formats used for creating content is a blog. A blog is a date-ordered list of articles (or posts) created by a single or small group of authors. Blogs are great for:

- Establishing expertise and experience
- Providing valuable and actionable information
- Achieving information leadership in your niche

Information leadership may sound like a fancy strategy for huge brands, but all it means is that because you share your expertise with your customers and prospective customers, they come to recognize you as an expert and they may even look forward to what you have to say next.

What Content Goes Into a Business Blog

For businesses this format can be very useful. But a blog used for business is very different than the typical personal blog and we use the term "business blog" to distinguish this type. A business blog should address three areas:

1. Feature objective content of interest to prospects and customers such as educational and usage information
2. Contain "qualifying content" or content that helps qualify a person based on their interest in the material
3. Build trust in the business

A business blog should be viewed as a work in progress with each new article adding value to customers and to your neighborhood brand.

What Goes Into a Blog Article?

Unlike a personal blog, a business blog should rarely, if ever, deal with thoughts or feelings. A business blog entry should:

- Stay within the expertise you represent
- Stress a single issue
- Be brief
- Use bulleted or numbered lists for clarity
- Be conversational (write as if talking to one person)
- Be personalized to provide a face behind the business
- Address your prospects, not friends and family

In order to come across as useful, blog posts should stay away from hard selling. The blog entry facilitates a sale by building trust. Let your online advertising and website close the deal. Remember, online tools need to work together and the only purpose of the blog is to build trust. Blog entries should avoid:

- Anything that seems like selling. A blog post is for information and building trust. Other tools work better for selling.
- Anything that assumes knowledge of specific recent events (remember users may be reading your blog post years into the

future, so write the content so that it can withstand the test of time).

Each blog entry should conclude with an invitation to comment. You may have forgotten something or may provoke a thought in your readers. They may want to share examples of their own. Encourage them to discuss and even debate the topic.

How Do You Start a Blog Article?

Creating content for a business blog entry takes time but it becomes easier with a good subject. A subject should not only focus the content but should also catch the reader's interest. Some good starting points often deal with a list of items or an answer to a question such as:

- 5 Ways to…
- 10 Reasons Why…
- 4 Examples of…
- 7 Habits of…
- 8 Websites That…
- How to…
- Why is…
- What should…

Then, simply list the answers to your title. Also consider these other sources for ideas:

- Last question asked by someone when they found out what your company did
- Last explanation you gave to a customer
- A question a customer asked the first time they came into your business
- How a current issue in the news is being addressed by your business

Writing regular blog posts may seem a little intimidating. But once you get started, you'll find that it isn't that hard because it's what you typically do every day – help customers. To get started, we suggest you sit down with your employees or a few customers and brainstorm a list of topics that would make good blog posts. Then, when it's time to write, grab a topic from your brainstorming list. Appendix C of this book provides a form you can use for writing down your brainstorms. With 20 topics in hand, you'll have almost a year's worth of blog posts ready to go with typically just an hour or two of effort for each article.

How a Blog Article is Judged

Readers determine the value of your blog post. They make this decision on a combination of factors including:

- Need – How relevant is the information to the user?
- Application – How easily can a reader apply the information?
- Clarity – Is the information easy to understand?
- Quality – Is the information grammatically correct?
- Results – Does the information answer the question?
- Resources – Does the topic promote further research through links?
- Title – Is the title an effective lead-in to the blog post? Will the words attract your target audience?

The higher the value of the blog entry, the more likely that readers will:

- See you as an expert
- Gain trust in your ability to address their needs
- Read the complete blog post
- Link to your content
- Share your content with their friends
- Comment and start a conversation

When readers do respond to your blog posts, it is important to reply promptly and treat the blog post as if it were an email. You will want to be sure the blog tool you use has a feature that alerts you by email when readers contribute their input.

Business blogging can take time, but as you stay with it over time, you build a base of content that benefits customers and your business. Appendix B of this guide provides a checklist for creating a blog post.

Email

Though email has been around longer than websites, it's surprising how few local businesses make good use of it. First, businesses need to understand that there are two types of email: email we want and email we don't. Even if an email message is not SPAM and there is permission to send it, it may still not be something that a reader wants. There is a golden rule of email and it states "Send only to others what you would want sent to you." Email also comes in two flavors — that which is personally written and that which is sent in bulk. Most people know the difference as soon as they look at it.

The golden rule doesn't mean that a business should send no email; it just means that the email it does send should be useful to the reader and sent infrequently enough so as not to be a nuisance. When these two rules are followed, email is a great tool to continue engagement with existing customers and maintain mindshare.

If you have a list of email addresses and are considering using them to send a bulk email, stop and consider how likely the recipient will consider the email as "junk". Here are some criteria on determining the value of your email list:

- How was the email list acquired? There is a vast difference between lists in which the contact provides you with an email address (known as an "opt-in" list) versus names obtained without the intended recipient's knowledge. The more permission your target list has granted you, the less likely your message will be seen as a nuisance.
- Is the recipient familiar with your business? The sender must be someone the reader already knows. Your message should clearly state who you are, what you do and how to contact you. This is especially important for first-time mailings.
- Is there an affinity between your business and the recipient? If you acquire a mailing list, you should use only those that have an affinity with your business. For example, people who have signed up for a parenting site are good candidates for educational toys, family vacations or low-cost/high-convenience items, like

books and CDs. But they are a poor choice for retirement condominiums, luxury cruises and cemetery plots. While that may sound like Marketing 101, too many groups act as if any email address is an appropriate email address.

- Is this an area in which the customer has expressed an interest? Again, like affinity groups, the more closely you can link your offer to known customer preferences, the more likely you are to conduct a successful mailing.

- If mailing to an in-house list, how long has it been since the last interaction with the customer? There's a fine line between informative and intrusive. When customers give you their email address, they are, in effect, granting you permission to talk to them. Do not abuse this permission. What they aren't agreeing to, however, is a continual bombardment of their inbox with all of your marketing and sales messages.

- Are there easy "opt-out" mechanisms in place for recipients who wish to remove themselves from future mailings? Just as you have the option of hanging up on a telephone solicitation, your recipients should also have the ability to easily "disconnect" themselves from your email campaign.

- Does your email contain something of value for your audience either in the content itself or from the website? A desire for greater sales is simply not a legitimate reason for bulk mailing. Savvy consumers always ask "what's in it for me?" If you can't answer that question, your efforts are doomed.

- Are you asking for money? The more blatant the request, the more spam-like the message. While it's acceptable to spotlight special or limited-time pricing, your message is much more likely to be read if cost is only part of the equation. Use other selling features, such as product benefits, customer testimonials, technical advantages, etc., as the crux of your message.

- Does the message have a valid reply address? It's hard to feel connected to a company when your only contact is with someone named "sales@company.com." Instead, use a real name. This helps personalize the message, making it less like spam and more like mail.

Using these criteria, businesses should readily address email contact with their customers. Personalized email is always preferred but bulk email works when it is not too frequent.

Once you send your email, be ready for replies. Your email campaign may start as a one-way effort, but the reply button can easily make it two-way and the sender will expect a quick and personal reply.

Beware Email Creation Effort

Bulk, or offer based, email can be as elaborate as any brochure and thus requires more preparation than the typical personal email we send every day. If you have a special event you want to market through email, consider engaging the services of a professional designer just as you would for creating a printed collateral piece. Also be sure and consider that not all email programs display email messages the same way. An email message that looks good when viewed in Google Gmail may not look good when displayed in Microsoft Outlook. Bulk email is considerably cheaper than postal mail, but it is not without cost or effort. Be sure you test your email message in different email programs before sending to everyone on your list.

Web Advertising

Advertisers have always sought efficient and effective ways to get their messages in front of customers and prospects. Over the centuries they have had to adapt to media formats that deliver their customers – whether it was newspapers, radio, television or magazines. Advertisers have always followed information or entertainment media and they continue to do so with the Internet.

The earliest web ads mimicked their magazine and newspaper forerunners in the form of banner advertising. This worked well when there were a few major web sites. Now the web consists of millions of sites, and users often turn to search engines. The online advertising landscape now includes:

- Banner advertising – Ads placed on websites that users visit that attempt to build awareness or click-throughs to a specific offer or website.
- Sponsored advertising – This is where, using something like

Google Adwords, advertisers compete and bid for search keywords so that when someone searches for a particular term their ad link shows up in the paid listings.

- Content advertising – Any type of web items such as web pages, articles, comments, photos, videos and files that show up in the primary list of search results. These results are also called the "organic" search results.

Each method of advertising has its advantages. Businesses should use each as appropriate in the framework of an overall neighborhood brand strategy.

Banner Advertising

Banner advertising has lost much of its effectiveness through overuse, but that doesn't mean it doesn't have a place in neighborhood advertising. Banner ads create awareness and help with key branding messages. The downside is that, for most banner ads, customers have to visit a website to see them. The increasing use of iPhones and other mobile browsers make website visits less frequent. To be effective, banner advertising must be pushed out to readers as well as being shown to website visitors.

A banner ad is a great place to start the neighborhood branding process because it can repeatedly drive home the name + niche part of the neighborhood brand equation. The more customers see your name with your specialty, the more likely they are to identify you with a problem they have. Like any other form of advertising, banner ads require consistent exposure and time to be effective.

Sponsored Advertising

Sponsored advertising has made Google what it is today, and if your customers find you primarily through Google search, then sponsored advertising is very effective. However, when targeting customers just a few blocks from your door, it may prove difficult to create keyword sponsorships that don't attract a large number of click-throughs (and costs) from outside the neighborhood.

Sponsored advertising can generate a click and awareness, but it isn't the best way to build a neighborhood brand or improve trust. Online, brand and trust are developed through content.

Content Advertising

Content advertising requires text that contains the keywords that people are likely to search for. Content advertising can be addressed through the effective use of websites, business blogs and other content distribution methods. Most businesses don't start with a large collection of content, but with consistent effort over a period of months businesses will find their content starting to show up in more and broader search results.

Web Public Relations

At one time, public relations, or PR, meant pitching editors and writers story ideas based on your business or product. While that is still true for larger companies with PR budgets, for smaller companies, PR is about creating content for automated news aggregation sites like Google or Yahoo news. For example if you go to Google news (http://news.google.com) and enter the query "organic trade association" you are presented a mix of articles and press releases. The press releases are not tied to a particular newspaper or magazine. Instead, they are tied directly to an online press newsroom. Google, Yahoo and many other news sites accumulate stories from these news sources and make their content searchable. Any service that subscribes to news feeds from Google or Yahoo receives these stories.

The main difference between traditional PR and web PR is that traditional PR is story oriented but web PR is keyword oriented. To get your press release into traditional media requires a good story. To get noticed in web PR your story needs to contain words and phrases that someone searches for. To increase your results be sure and include in your story references to things, people or businesses that you know, service, sell or provide assistance to. With that as background, there are many activities that are newsworthy and candidates for press releases including:

- New customer
- Customer usage profile

- New location or expansion
- Community activities such as donations, sponsorships or underwriting
- New merchandise lines or services
- Awards and recognitions
- Interesting or innovative customer experiences
- Speaking appearances

When composing a press release for the web, keep in mind the following:

- Choose a keyword phrase for your story that is likely to be searched
- Repeat the keyword phrase in your title and several times within the article
- Make sure the title is engaging and descriptive
- Make sure the press release is newsworthy and will help your branding efforts. Whenever possible include customer references and quotes
- Include URLs that help identify specific information about your company or customers that are mentioned
- Include a phone number and email address
- Include your location, zip code, city and neighborhood in the article
- Be descriptive for first-time readers as well as search engines

Just because your business is small and you don't use a professional PR firm, don't assume that your story won't get picked up by traditional media sites. Almost every journalist today now uses the Internet for research and story ideas. When journalists or customers are searching for news about your area or a particular business specialty, a web PR effort makes it easier for them to find you.

Social Networking Tools

Social networking is people talking to people. It is not a new concept. Before the web, and still today, there are church socials, bridge parties, playgroups and a whole variety of ways that people get together to share details about their lives and thoughts about their neighborhood. Social networking is the same on the web. However, for neighborhood businesses, the changes in brand velocity, the speed with which your brand is communicated to others, is staggering.

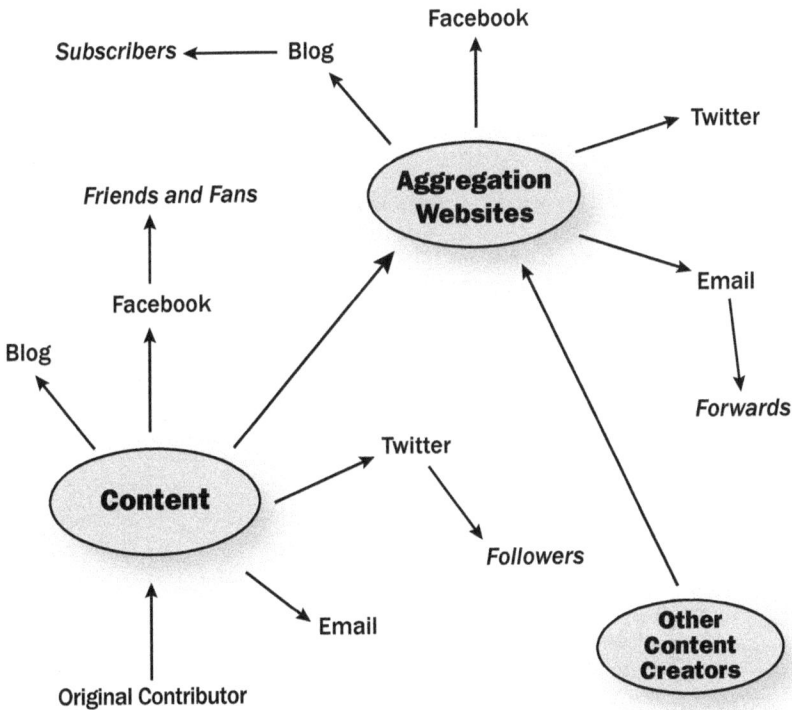

Figure 14 – Social Media Connections

During the church social era, a good or bad story made the rounds over days, weeks or months. Now it can happen in minutes. Services like Facebook make news almost instant among friends and family. With concepts like email forwarding, Facebook replies and Twitter "retweets", stories can very quickly and effortlessly spread to a large number of people.

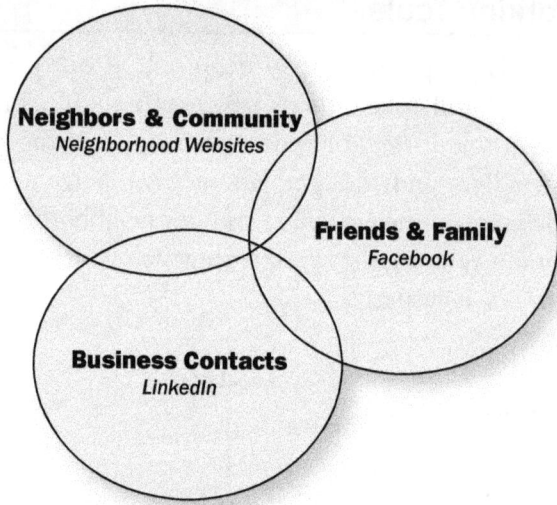

Figure 15 – Social Media Universe

Although many people equate social marketing with Facebook, Facebook addresses only one part of online socialization due to its level of assumed intimacy between relationships. Based on how much we want to share, other social networking platforms also make sense. The following chart summarizes this better.

Figure 16 – Social Media Intimacy

Facebook now has Fan pages that require less intimacy, but any time businesses are communicating with the customers through their "walls", they need to take more care and assume a higher level of customer trust. It is a mark of trust to be allowed to post a someone's Facebook wall and there is fine line between getting exposure and being instrusive.

Neighborhood Website

We have a friend who complains that Facebook doesn't have a "sort of friends" category. With Facebook it's all or nothing regardless of the closeness of the connection. This makes it great for good friends and family, but less than ideal for people down the street. Plus with Facebook, you have to know the person's name in order to form the connection. Neighborhoods don't work this way.

A neighborhood website has two key features:

1. It's a place that has very specific geographic or community focus
2. It's a place where members learn about, discuss and share with other neighbors or community members any information about neighborhood matters

Neighborhood sites typically originate around a local newspaper trying to repurpose its news or an off-the-shelf solution designed around blogging. Banner ads from local business then drive the site's revenue. These sites often feature:

- Proprietary news from a single source
- A community blog where one or more people discuss events

These sites are visitor-oriented in that they expect readers to continually visit the website to keep track of what's new or changed since the last time. They are usually dependent on a handful of people for content that suffers when these people move or go on vacation. Think of these approaches as Neighborhood Websites version 1.0. They are the majority of current sites and are driven more by the content or the off-the-shelf technology than the actual make-up of a neighborhood.

Introducing Neighborhood Websites 2.0

If you look closely at any neighborhood you'll see groups. If you think about it, we generally come to know our neighbors not based on where our house is, but by what groups within the neighborhood we belong to. Kid's classrooms, churches, scout troops and other volunteer and civic groups make more of a difference on who we know than who lives down the street.

If you look a little broader you'll continue to see groups based around local businesses as well. There are groups of people we continually run into where we shop or eat. Sometimes they are the people who work there and often they are the other customers we run into when we visit. You add these all up and what you'll find is that a neighborhood is really a group-of-groups centered on a common geography.

In order to address this group-of-groups neighborhood makeup, a new type of neighborhood website is emerging that can be described as Neighborhood Websites 2.0. In 2.0 the neighborhood site:

- Provides group tools that enable discussions and sharing within a smaller group or within the larger neighborhood group
- Provides groups for different needs such as sports teams, business blogs or school projects
- Collects neighborhood news from a wide variety of sources
- Allows group members to participate with each other
- Allows groups to share or "bubble" information with other groups
- Participation in one group benefits the overall community
- Doesn't rely on a small group of individuals for ongoing success and new content
- Allows local businesses to have their own groups side by side with other neighborhood groups
- Uses email, Twitter and other distribution methods to push content to the readers rather than relying on "revisits" to a website

The reason a business locates in a neighborhood is because that is where the customers are. This same rule applies to online efforts as well. Local businesses need to be where their customers are.

When creating content and placing ads, there are numerous opportunities on a national level. Yet being one of the millions of blogs or URLs on the web can make a business the proverbial needle in the haystack for potential customers. Better to be the big man on a small campus than an unknown on a larger one. This is where a neighborhood website can make a huge difference to a local business.

Facebook

If you don't already have a personal Facebook account, then you are one of a rapidly shrinking number. While Facebook may have started as a service for college kids, it now has gone mainstream. It now has more than 400 million users worldwide (more by the time you read this) with more than 36% of all users over the age of 35 and 60% over the age of 25. More than 55% of all Facebook users are women.

There is no better way to stay in touch with a large number of friends and family across time zones and continents than Facebook. When I went off to college, many years ago, I left behind my high school friends for new college friends, though not by choice. I just couldn't stay in touch. Now when my kids go to college, they take their high school friends with them on Facebook. And, I've watched this trend continue through each major life change such as career and family.

For businesses, both neighborhood and not, this means that one customer represents many more. Give customers a good story and you may find that story accelerated as fast as they can type on their phones. For a neighborhood business, the downside is that a great story about a local bakery won't help much with friends in other states. However, Facebook provides a concept called "fan pages" that helps businesses build their own Facebook friends.

The concept of a fan page is simple. You create a fan page for your business and then encourage other Facebook users to become fans. Then when you post something on the wall of your fan page, it instantly appears on the walls of your fans. More interestingly, this message is also viewable by the friends of your fans. The more fans you have, the more fans and friends of fans you reach.

While fan pages sound great, businesses need to experiment with their usage. They are subject to overuse. Just as it is easy for someone to become a fan of your business, it is also easy for them to stop being a fan. Posting the right messages and on a not too frequent schedule is something that each business needs to address.

Twitter

Twitter is a micro-blogging site that, like a regular blog site, lets users make posts and then automatically distribute those posts to interested readers with one exception – blog entries are limited to 140 characters and can contain only text. While it seems that 140 characters would be a huge limitation, it forces people to communicate only the most basic information or summary of information.

Twitter has its own vocabulary and it helps to understand some of the terms before going into more detail: Common Twitter terms are:

- Tweet – An individual Twitter message
- Tweeter – A user who has an account at Twitter allowing them to send and subscribe to Twitter messages
- Follower – A person who subscribes to receive Twitter messages from others
- @Replies – A twitter message directed to a single user but available for all to see
- #Hashtag – A word preceded by the pound sign that helps improve searching across Tweets
- Retweet – A tweet read by one follower that is forwarded on to his or her followers
- Tiny URL – Since some URLs can be quite long, several web services have been created whose purpose is to take a long URL, save it, and then provide a reference to that URL that is much shorter
- GeoTweet – A Tweet that also includes a Tweeter's location information. GeoTweets can be generated by phones with built-in GPS functions
- Lists – A list of Twitter users that can be collectively referenced by one list name rather that by each individual user name
- Twitter client – a program that runs on a computer or phone that enables someone to send/read tweets

Twitter content is highly searchable on the Twitter website or using one of the many Twitter clients by:

- Word
- Sender
- Hashtag
- Location

Tweets are now picked up by search engines and therefore they add to a business' web content.

LinkedIn

LinkedIn has become the dominant way of connecting to your business contacts, both past and present. It provides a way to stay in touch with everyone you've met, or worked or done business with. Neighborhood businesses that deliver professional services should have an active presence on LinkedIn.

LinkedIn is about networking. By linking to other LinkedIn users you define your network of business contacts and customers. Then as you update your LinkedIn status, your information is broadcast to your network. Through your network, you can get referrals and introductions to people in the networks of your contacts. This makes LinkedIn a good way for finding new contacts as well as staying in front of existing ones.

Integrating Online and Offline Branding

Although this chapter is near the end of the book, there is very good reason it should be at the beginning. And that reason is that your Internet efforts start offline in your store or business. Every conversation that starts offline should be continued online. Your online efforts are a natural extension of your in-store efforts and your in-store efforts are a natural extension of your online efforts. The two work hand-in-hand to engage and re-engage customers.

To build and enhance your neighborhood brand, you need to facilitate stories for customers to tell others. These stories lead to new customers and repeat business. The best way to do this is to engage online. But to engage online, you need to know who your customers are and how to reach them. On the Internet, this is typically their email address.

Engagement Generation vs. Lead Generation

Most people understand the concept of lead generation. That is you solicit names of prospects and then attempt to close them for new business. If the lead doesn't close, the name is discarded and new leads are solicited and the process repeated. On the Internet, this process is considerably different, think of it as engagement generation.

In engagement generation, prospects and customers are asked to join your business in one or more of the following online areas:

- Email list
- Blog subscriber
- Facebook fan
- Twitter follower
- LinkedIn contact
- Website member for access to photos or special content

Then, when they are a part of your online community you carefully build the relationship over time and attempt to move the contact to higher levels of engagement. There are several techniques proven effective to obtain a customer's email address:

- Ask them directly
- Provide access to information (Product support information, white papers)
- Give discounts (email coupon, notice of special sales)
- Send follow-ups (check up on their product usage and satisfaction)
- Provide electronic receipts (send invoices)
- Offer reminders (appointments)

Remember, engaging online is much less expensive than trying to reach customers through advertising. There is no reason to spend good money trying to find people through search advertising when you have already had them inside your store.

From a customer standpoint, advertising and online options make the world a noisy place. It is easy for a business to lose a customer through forgetfulness and distraction. Businesses can no longer assume that if someone visits or purchases once, they will be back – even if they had a good experience. That's why it's important to engage with your customers, continue the relationship and maintain your mindshare with them. This can increase customer loyalty to your brand.

Neighborhood Brand Consistency

Do you have that piece of clothing your sister-in-law might have given you at Christmas that you just can't bring yourself to wear because it's not YOU? We all have a fairly well developed sense of our own personal style, and others also associate us with particular patterns of dressing, interacting, etc. They notice when for whatever reason we don't look like ourselves. Disjointed, brand messages that don't match are just as out of place as that holiday sweater. Whether consumers will muster the courage to tell you or not, they DO notice branding inconsistencies.

To professional marketers, this idea of consistency is known as Integrated Marketing Communications (IMC). It is the idea that branding messages are discernible in everything you do, from the shingle hanging in front of your business to your telephone message, how you greet your customers, how your sales staff answers questions, the tone of your emails, your choice of colors, your packaging style, your blog demeanor, etc. These messages solidify your neighborhood brand. The guiding principle for integrating online and offline branding is to have all branding efforts say the same thing.

If you are accustomed to using only print advertising in newspapers or magazines, achieving integration with your ad messaging may result from simply comparing your ads side by side and assessing whether they look consistent or fit together well. This seamless concept and message integration across all customer "touchpoints," as they are sometimes called, requires that you maintain consistency at every turn.

Does Your Store Match Your Brand?

To take this idea of comparison to another level, take your advertising and walk outside your store and hold it up so that you can compare your advertising with your store front. Is there still a match? Hold the advertisement while talking to your staff. Is there still a match? For a neighborhood brand, all your online and offline elements should match.

When you are planning your budget, your website probably ends up under marketing expense. But, like your website, other elements that affect the customer experience should be included as well. Consider the following list as neighborhood brand marketing expenses if you don't already:

- Store appearance
- Phone or handwritten follow-ups
- Staff training

If you've integrated your online and offline efforts successfully your customers won't really notice the transition in either direction. The better the offline experience, the more receptive customers are to your online efforts.

Implementing a Neighborhood Branding Strategy

In this guide, we've tried to layout the basic information you need to use the Internet to build your neighborhood brand. The guide has outlined the information needed to define a strategy based around:

1. Using web content targeted at search engines and customers to build a neighborhood brand.
2. Leveraging social networks and neighborhood communities to accelerate your brand.

The following checklist summarizes this material in some concrete tasks. While each business will implement each task differently, the checklist should be a good place to start.

Getting Started

❑ Fill in the blank: When customers think about _____, I want them to think about my business.

❑ Identify and refine your neighborhood niche.

❑ Develop customer profile.

Web Basics

- ❑ Set up website.
- ❑ Set up business blog.
- ❑ Set up Facebook Fan page (as appropriate).
- ❑ Set up Twitter account (as appropriate).
- ❑ Set up LinkedIn account (as appropriate).

Cross Promotion / Engagement Generation

- ❑ Implement in-store email collection.
- ❑ Implement in-store web sign-up blog, Fan page, Twitter, LinkedIn.
- ❑ Invite current email list to sign up.
- ❑ Implement advertising and other activities to generate awareness.

Ongoing

- ❑ Start regular blog posts.
- ❑ Start regular posts to Facebook and Twitter.
- ❑ Start regular status updates on LinkedIn.
- ❑ Visit the website http://www.neighborhoodmarketing101.com for additional resources.

Working through these checklists may pose time or skill problems that are difficult to get past. The next chapter provides some ways to get started without changing your daily focus.

Getting Started

Becoming a neighborhood brand isn't complicated, but it does take time and consistency. Good intentions often conflict with reality and building your brand or "marketing" frequently takes a back seat to selling and delivering. Yet, most business owners know they need to market.

Sadly, one of the biggest impediments to marketing may be the lack of results businesses have achieved through prior efforts. Traditional marketing opportunities have typically had a guaranteed cost but never a guaranteed result. This is why neighborhood branding is so different from traditional marketing. With neighborhood branding, it isn't about what others do for your business; it's about what you do for your business.

Why Tools Are Important

Few people would start trying to build a house with just a hammer and a hand saw. Though just those two tools could be used to build a house, the amount of time it would take would be beyond most people's schedule. That's also the way it is with neighborhood branding – the right tools can simplify and speed the process.

To reach neighborhood customers and prospects typically requires businesses to utilize a variety of dissimilar tools to get the job done. Facebook, Google, LinkedIn, Twitter, blogging, websites and other ways of reaching customers all have their own setup and administration which makes using more than one of them often time prohibitive. But to reach customers, businesses can't depend on just one of these tools; they need to use all of them. This is a problem created by technology that can actually be solved by technology.

While there are a variety of tools neighborhood businesses can use, this book is heavily biased towards the use of the Neighborhood Marketing Center provided by BubbleLife Media. Neighborhood Marketing Center is an online solution that provides:

1. Content management for blogging and organizing articles, events and other online information.

2. Member management for centralizing customer contact information.

3. Distribution capabilities for getting content to customers, social media sites and the neighborhood.

4. Reporting and analytics tools to see what's working and what needs changing.

Beyond the powerful features Neighborhood Marketing Center offers for any business, perhaps its biggest strength is that it is tied closely to a neighborhood website through http://www.bubblelife.com. The neighborhood websites available through bubblelife.com feature the latest capabilities as described previously in this book as Neighborhood Websites 2.0. Content created in the Neighborhood Marketing Center can be easily distributed through the neighborhood website to the entire neighborhood database of readers and followers.

Why Expertise is Important

While Neighborhood Marketing Center makes it easy to implement neighborhood branding, it won't work if it doesn't get used consistently. BubbleLife Media and other marketing consultants can help you utilize the Neighborhood Marketing Center on a regular basis to touch your customers and prospects without taking up much time. Plus, the benefits of using a fully integrated tool, like Neighborhood Marketing Center, means that hourly or monthly charges are kept to a minimum.

Beyond the "getting it done" factor, outside expertise can also help a business with issues such as:

- Topics
- Writing skills
- Artwork and photography
- Latest techniques and trends

Most people look to a local business for their expertise on a product, selection or service rather than their Facebook skills. For example, most customers prefer their dentists to read the latest dental publications rather than books on how to market on Facebook. Outside expertise can help neighborhood businesses grow and stay focused on what they do best.

For More Information

Visit BubbleLife Media's website at http://www.bubblelifemedia.com to learn more or visit http://www.bubblelife.com to see neighborhood branding in action.

About the Authors

Jeff Farris

Jeff Farris is a Managing Partner with BubbleLife Media. Previously he was the founder in 1997 of e2 Communications, a provider of email marketing communications. As President and Chief Executive Officer, Mr. Farris led e2 Communications to become the recognized technology leader with a global customer base of over 400 customers. e2 Communications was sold in 2001.

Prior to e2 Communications, Mr. Farris was the founder in 1988 of Saber Software Corporation, a developer of network systems management software. Under Mr. Farris' leadership as President and Chief Executive Officer, Saber Software ranked number 26 of Inc. Magazine's list of Fastest Growing Private Companies in 1993. Mr. Farris led Saber Software to a successful initial public offering in 1994 and positioned the company to become the industry leader for network systems management products according to IDC. Saber was acquired by Network Associates (McAfee) in 1995. In 1994, the year prior to its acquisition, Saber Software reached $20 million in worldwide annual sales.

Dr. Alice Kendrick

Alice Kendrick, Ph.D is professor of advertising in the Temerlin Advertising Institute at Southern Methodist University. Her research about advertising effectiveness and place branding has appeared in national and international academic journals as well as the advertising trade press. She is co-author of two books, Successful Advertising Research Methods and Advertising's War on Terror, for which she received the Great Minds Research Innovation Award from the Advertising Research Foundation. She is also the recipient of the Carl Rosenfeld Education Prize for her research and writing on the effectiveness of promotional products.

Alice currently serves as a public member of the National Advertising Review Board, and has served as a consultant for local and national organizations including Texas Instruments, Carrington Laboratories, The Richards Group, American Cyanamid, The American Advertising Federation, Promotional Products Association International, Guaranty Federal Bank, and Seccion Amarilla US.

Appendix A
Website Content Checklist

Every business is different but there are similarities when it comes to what customers and search engines expect from a website. The overall mission of a website is to support your neighborhood brand and help customers quickly connect and create the stories they'll need to reinforce and repeat your brand to others. It should stress the business' core message and neighborhood location.

Below is a checklist of content that helps a website become a destination for customers and content for search engines. Not all items apply to all businesses, but the list should help you think about your own needs.

Calls to Action

- ❑ Join Our Group/Email List
- ❑ Become a Facebook Fan
- ❑ Follow Us on Twitter
- ❑ Download Our Whitepaper

Dynamic Content

- ❑ News or Blog Updates
- ❑ Calendar Information

Product and Category Information

- [ ] Brands
- [ ] Usage Information
- [ ] Store Support Information
- [ ] Manufacturer Support Information
- [ ] Links to Helpful Resources

Reference Information

- [ ] Reference Customers
- [ ] Customer Testimonials
- [ ] Recent Transactions
- [ ] Support for Neighborhood Causes and Groups

General Contact Information

- [ ] Physical Address
- [ ] Phone Numbers
- [ ] Email Addresses
- [ ] Facebook Link
- [ ] Twitter Link
- [ ] LinkedIn Link

Business Information

- [ ] Physical Address
- [ ] Hours of Operation
- [ ] Map
- [ ] Pictures of Exterior
- [ ] Pictures of Interior
- [ ] Company History

Management and Staff Information

- [ ] Names, Titles, Backgrounds and Pictures
- [ ] Contact Information

Search Engine Information

- [ ] Page Title
- [ ] Meta Description
- [ ] Meta Tags
- [ ] Use of HTML Headings for Key Phrases
- [ ] Words Used in Searches

Appendix B
New Content Checklist

Use this checklist for blog posts or event comments on blog posts on other sites. Keep in mind the following questions:

1. Does the content enhance my status as an expert in my business?
2. Is the content relevant to my desired customers?
3. If a customer forwards this blog post to a friend, will the friend gain trust in my business or services?

Then make sure each of the following checklist items are completed.

Focus

- ❑ Intriguing Title
- ❑ Single Topic

Writing Style

- ❑ Good First Sentence (for summaries)
- ❑ Short Sentences
- ❑ Few Paragraphs
- ❑ Bulleted or Numbered Lists (if possible)

Quality Control

- ❑ Spell Checked
- ❑ Fact Checked

Reader Viewpoint

- ❑ Useful
- ❑ Applicable
- ❑ Understandable (clear idea, simple terminology)

Conclusion

- ❑ Call to Comment
- ❑ Signature with link to URL, email address, phone, etc.

Content Survey

If time permits, consider showing you blog post to a few customers for their feedback. A standard list of questions might include:

1. What was the first thing that came to your mind when you read this article?
2. In your own words, what is the main message that this article is trying to communicate to you?
3. Does this article cause you to see (your business) as better than other competitors?
4. Is there anything confusing or hard to believe about this article? If yes, what?

Have them answer the following questions on a range of 1 to 5.

	1	2	3	4	5	
Difficult to understand						Easy to understand
Not interesting						Interesting
Not believable						Believable
Not trustworthy						Trustworthy
Not useful						Useful
Inappropriate						Appropriate
Dull						Creative
Would never pass along						Would share with friend

If you score below a 4 on any single item, you should consider revising your approach.

Appendix C
Business Blog Brainstorm

List 20 topics that you can use for your upcoming articles. Then, post every 2-3 weeks.

Working Title	Specific Content Ideas
Example: 5 Ways to Come Up with Blog Titles	Questions, News Stories, New Product, Usage Information
1.	
2.	
3.	
4.	
5.	
6	

Working Title	Specific Content Ideas
7.	
8.	
9.	
10.	
11.	
12.	
13.	
14.	
15.	
16,	
17.	
18.	
19.	
20.	

www.ingramcontent.com/pod-product-compliance
Lightning Source LLC
Chambersburg PA
CBHW031814190326
41518CB00006B/328